SPERM
WHALES

Printed in Hong Kong

98 99 00 01 02 5 4 3 2 1

Library of Congress Cataloging-in-Publication Data
Sperm whales / Jonathan Gordon.
p.   cm. — (World life library)
ISBN 0-89658-398-8
I. Sperm whale. I. Title. II. Series.
QL737.C435G67 1998   98-18528
599.5'47–dc21   CIP

Distributed in Canada by Raincoast Books, 8680 Cambie Street, Vancouver, B.C. V6P 6M9

Published by Voyageur Press, Inc.
123 North Second Street, P. O. Box 338, Stillwater, MN 55082 U.S.A.
651-430-2210, fax 651-430-2211

Educators, fundraisers, premium and gift buyers, publicists and marketing managers:
Looking for creative products and new sales ideas? Voyageur Press books are available at special
discounts when purchased in quantities, and special editions can be created to your
specifications. For details contact the marketing department at 800-888-9653.

Photographs copyright © 1998 by

Front cover © François Gohier
Back cover © Barbara Todd
Page 1 © François Gohier
Page 4 © A.N.T. (NHPA)
Page 6 © François Gohier
Page 9 © François Gohier
Page 10 © Howard Hall (Oxford Scientific Films)
Page 11 © François Gohier
Page 12 © Stewart Aitchison/Okapia (Oxford Scientific Films)
Page 13 © Flip Nicklin (Minden Pictures)
Page 15 © Flip Nicklin (Minden Pictures)
Page 16 © François Gohier
Page 19 © Flip Nicklin (Minden Pictures)
Page 20 © François Gohier

Page 23 © François Gohier
Page 24 © Flip Nicklin (Minden Pictures)
Page 27 © François Gohier
Page 28 © Flip Nicklin (Minden Pictures)
Page 30 © Mark Carwardine (Still Pictures)
Page 31 © François Gohier
Page 32 © François Gohier
Page 35 © Flip Nicklin (Minden Pictures)
Page 36 © François Gohier
Page 38 © Mark Carwardine (Still Pictures)
Page 39 © François Gohier
Page 40 © Michael Leach (NHPA)
Page 43 © François Gohier
Page 44 © *Song of the Whale* Research IFAW

Page 47 © François Gohier
Page 48 © *Song of the Whale* Research IFAW
Page 51 © Flip Nicklin (Minden Pictures)
Page 52 © Flip Nicklin (Minden Pictures)
Page 55 © François Gohier
Page 56 © *Song of the Whale* Research IFAW
Page 59 © *Song of the Whale* Research IFAW
Page 60 © François Gohier
Page 63 © Flip Nicklin (Minden Pictures)
Page 64 © François Gohier
Page 67 © François Gohier
Page 68 © Flip Nicklin (Minden Pictures)
Page 70 © François Gohier

SPERM
WHALES

Jonathan Gordon

Voyageur Press

Contents

The Sperm Whale

By any measure, the sperm whale is a most magnificent animal. Few other species, even amongst the great whales, can lay claim to such an impressive array of extreme statistics and unique records and many of these will be explored in this book. Sperm whales are the largest of the toothed whales, with males reaching lengths of over 60 ft (18 m). They are also the most sexually dimorphic of cetaceans. At less than 40 ft (12 m) the females are only two thirds of the length, and one third of the mass, of the males. Sperm whales are the most accomplished of mammalian divers, reaching depths of over 6560 ft (2000 m) and are able to remain submerged for over an hour. They are extremely vocal animals, making powerful clicks for most of the time that they are underwater. Over a third of their bodies is given over to sound production and they carry the world's largest natural sound-producing organ in their massive heads. Sperm whales are also the most social of the great whales, and perhaps most intriguingly of all, they have the largest brains that have ever existed.

Although they have a very low reproductive rate, the lowest of any animal, sperm whales have a large world population and a wide geographical range. They are found in deep water in all of the world's oceans, ranging from the Arctic through the tropical seas to the Antarctic. In spite of this, they were, until recently, rarely seen alive and the study of the behavior of live sperm whales is a very recent undertaking.

Many aspects of the animal's biology and its natural behavior may remain poorly known, but the image of a sperm whale is a familiar one. Most whale caricatures and cartoons are based on it and many, who have never even been to sea, have at least been introduced to a sperm whale through reading *Moby Dick*.

The ancestors of the sperm whales, like those of all whales and dolphins, were land mammals. Some 52 million years ago, in the shallow waters fringing the Tethys Sea (an ancient ocean whose modern remnants are the Mediterranean and the

A sperm whale's unusual and highly adapted body conceals many mysteries and secrets.

Arabian Gulf), creatures that were the ancestors of the modern whales and dolphins began to diverge from animals that would eventually evolve into the modern even-toed ungulates (cows, sheep etc). These earliest whales, the Archaeocetes, probably evolved a marine way of life to exploit abundant food resources in the ancient oceans, possibly filling niches left by the giant, whale-like, sea-going reptiles. The adaptation of a land-based, four-legged body plan to a streamlined, fish-like body, propelled through water by a broad horizontal tail is one of the most obviously dramatic examples of evolution in the animal kingdom. Of course, these changes in the animals' body shape were paralleled by equally profound changes in their physiology; those allowing them to become breath-hold divers and to survive in a salty sea without drinking fresh water, for example, and by changes in their sensory systems, away from a reliance on smell, vision and in-air hearing towards a dependence on underwater sound. Animals that were recognizably sperm whales appeared relatively quickly, with the earliest fossils dating back some 23 million years, making sperm whales one of the most ancient of living cetacean families. The major division in the cetacea is between the toothed whales and the baleen whales. Sperm whales do seem distinct from other toothed whales in many ways, but with their teeth, single blowholes and asymmetrical skulls, anatomical observations seem to place them squarely in the toothed-whale camp. Recent genetic evidence, however, suggests that sperm whales may, in fact, be more closely related to the baleen whales than to other toothed whales. This unexpected suggestion remains a matter of heated debate and consensus on the sperm whale's proper place within cetacean systematics has yet to be reached.

The sperm whale's most prominent feature is its head. It is an enormous structure, accounting for up to a third of the total body length in mature males. At its apex, in the top left-hand corner, is the blowhole. S-shaped when closed, it opens into a wide oval each time the whale breathes. The head is like two fused barrels,

Caught in mid air with only its flukes still in the water, a sperm whales breaches off the Azores.

*Left alone in the sunlit surface waters off the Caribbean Island of Dominica when
its mother dived to feed, this curious calf inspects a photographer. The remoras on its back are
harmless scavengers and are typically found on calves (perhaps because they can't withstand the deep
dives of the adults). The pronounced wrinkling on the rear part of the animal's body can be clearly seen.*

set one above the other and thrusting forwards to overhang the upper jaw. A slight crease runs backwards between the bulge of each 'barrel' towards the eye which is just above the angle of the jaw. The skin of the head is beautifully smooth, like most of the rest of the body it is a gray or a chocolate-brown color, depending on the light. Mature males often carry long, white parallel scars on their heads, thought to be from deep tooth rakes inflicted by other males during fights. The heads of mature males may become almost completely white with accumulated scars.

Below the head is slung a long c10 ft (c3 m) thin lower jaw. Sperm whales can open their lower jaws wide, to about 90°, and with its fine profile, the jaw seems adapted to being snapped shut quickly. The lower jaw may look fragile but the bone within it, the mandible, is dense, as thick as a man's arm and immensely strong.

A sperm whale's head with its single blowhole offset to the left.

The lower jaw carries 20 to 25 pairs of large peg-like teeth. Each is planted firmly within a socket in the mandible. These may grow up to 10 in (25 cm) and weigh over 2 lb (1 kg). When the jaw shuts each tooth fits neatly into its own socket in the upper jaw. The teeth of the upper jaw, by contrast, are virtually absent, being represented by rudimentary stumps at the top of each socket. Interestingly, the teeth of the lower jaw don't erupt until well after young sperm whales have begun to take food, and in some females they don't emerge at all. Their role may have more to do with competition, especially between males, than with nutrition.

The skin around the mouth typically has a pale coloration so that sperm whales can seem to have white lips. The inside of the mouth is a reddish-pink suggesting that it is well vascularized. Sperm whales have a long muscular tongue, which, it is supposed, serves to manipulate prey and maneuver them into the whale's throat. Close examination of the skin around the jaws reveals round scars from the suckers of squid, testament to their last despairing grasp as they disappear down the whale's gullet. Unlike that of the plankton-eating baleen whales, the sperm whale's throat is capacious, wide enough, in fact, for a man to pass down it. Indeed, in the days of open-boat whaling this fate overtook a few unfortunate souls when enraged whales turned on their tormentors.

A sperm whale blowing at the surface off Mexico.

Passing back down the body, above and behind the angle of the jaw, we find the eye. The eye seems small by comparison with the size of the rest of the body but, in fact, it is about 2½ in (6 cm) in diameter, making it larger than most mammalian eyes. Since the functioning of the eye depends on its absolute, not its relative, size there is every reason to believe that the sperm whale's sense of vision is very good. The eyes are situated on slight bulges, even so, sperm whales have difficulty seeing past the great mass of their heads. Indeed, it seems that their best vision is forwards and downwards. I have often been in the water when an inquisitive sperm whale has swum over to investigate. The typical sequence of events is for it to echolocate from a distance of 165 ft (50 m) or more while swimming towards you. You can literally 'feel' the rapid clicks hitting your body as the approaching whale interrogates it with sound! Getting closer the whale will usually dive underneath you while turning so that its belly is towards you and it can have a good look, using both eyes in stereo, without the rest of its head getting in the way.

The characteristic blow of a sperm whale, low, bushy and
deflected to the left. At the surface sperm whales look stiff, like floating
logs. The swelling towards the front of the animal overlies the spermacetic organ.

Like all cetaceans, sperm whales have no external ears, but just behind the eye is the 'auditory meatus', a narrow channel leading towards the eardrum. This is so small that it is difficult to find, even on a dead whale. In fact the channel itself is occluded and it isn't an important pathway for sound to reach the ear. Underwater, sound can readily travel through the whale's body. The area around the auditory meatus is one preferred pathway for sound to reach the inner ear, and it is thought that another important acoustic route to the ear in toothed whales is through the lower jaw which contains a special fatty sound channel leading to the ear. The inner ears lie close to the cranium which contains the whale's brain. At 20 lb (9 kg) it is the largest brain on the planet, and highly adapted for acoustic processing.

The sperm whale's large, paddle-shaped pectoral fins mark the widest part of the body. These, of course, are homologous with our own arms and are used to provide steerage and maneuverability rather than propulsion. There are no hind limbs in cetaceans, they are reduced to a few vestiges hidden deep within the body.

From here aft, the body tapers away gradually to the tail and is dominated by massive blocks of muscles; the great natural powerhouses that drive the sperm whale's huge tail-flukes. These muscles have a definition that would be the envy of any body-builder, and to see them working, flexing the whale's body up and down to drive the flukes, is an awe-inspiring sight. Whales and dolphins, of course, move their flukes vertically in contrast to fish, which flex them from side to side. Whales' flukes are wonderful structures; they contain no bone, being mainly composed of arrays of connective tissue. Sperm whale flukes are the largest, in proportion to body size, of any cetaceans and are remarkably flexible, especially when compared with the stiff flukes of the baleen whales. They seem adapted for achieving relatively slow but highly efficient movement through the water.

The after part of the sperm whale's body is unusual in being pitted with a network of smooth indentations and creases. The function of this is unclear but it has been suggested that perhaps, rather like the dimples in a golf ball, these may reduce hydrodynamic drag.

'In no living thing are the lines of beauty more exquisitely defined
than in the crescentic borders of these flukes. At its utmost expansion in the full
grown whale, the tail will considerably exceed twenty feet across.' Herman Melville, Moby Dick.

Social Behavior & Family Life

The uninterrupted ocean world inhabited by sperm whales contains few obvious landmarks. In this always-changing, yet monotonously constant, blueness it is other sperm whales, and the social groups they form, that provide the one ever-present, stable feature in their lives.

Sperm whales are the most social of the great whales. The fundamental social units for sperm whales are called 'mixed groups' and consist of mature females and young of both sexes. A typical mixed social group may have 20 or so members, but within any group there will be complex patterns of association and preferred partnerships, probably reflecting the histories and structures of the families that make it up. These groups are thought to be based on matrilines: family groups of grandmothers, their daughters and grandchildren. Associations between some individuals are known to last many years, and probably extend over decades, but it is relatively rare to see all the members of a group close together on the surface at one time. Usually, the group members will be spread out over an area of tens of square miles foraging on their own or in small groups of two or three. They probably spread out like this to avoid interfering with each other while foraging. However, about once a day, the whales in a school stop feeding and aggregate into one or more large groups at the surface for an hour or two. During these periods they seem to be resting (there may be physiological reasons to do with diving which mean they have to spend some time resting each day). They also seem to spend a great deal of time 'socializing'. Perhaps because of the presence of their school-mates, they seem relaxed and tolerant of human swimmers and, as they are also close to the surface, this is one occasion when we can observe them underwater to actually see what they are doing beneath the surface. These all-too-brief, exhilarating glimpses reveal deeply social animals. In spite of their great size,

Companions, like members of this social group, are a constant feature in the life of sperm whales.

they move gracefully and gently around each other: their buoyancy is perfectly controlled. They seem to love to touch each other, often rolling along each other's bodies in what can seem like an underwater dance. One practical effect of this is to rub off great sheets of skin. Sperm whales slough their skin continuously, the reason may be to prevent fouling by marine organisms; certainly their bodies are remarkably clean and smooth. Their jaws seem to be particularly important areas, and it is not unusual to see animals gently clasping jaws. One of the revelations of these glimpses of sperm whale family life is just how timid these awesome animals seem to be. They can be easily scared by human swimmers, and are at best tolerant of their presence, usually moving away. More surprising, is to see how dolphins – one per cent the sperm whales' mass – appear to harass and upset them, sometimes even seeming to face down and see off the largest predator on earth.

During these social periods the whales are very vocal, but rather than making their usual monotonous 'regular' clicks, they produce clicks in discrete stereotyped patterns, called codas, which we believe are used for communication. This is also a time when sperm whales engage in more flamboyant above-water behaviors, for example, 'breaching', when a whale swims quickly up to the surface so that most of its body shoots clear into the air before tumbling back with a tremendous splash and a welter of foam, or 'lobtailing', when a whale brings its flukes up above the surface before smashing them down on the water with a resounding crash that can make the water 'smoke'. These two displays certainly serve as reminders of their size and power. In the days of whaling, boats were smashed to matchwood by lobtailing whales and the awe-struck sailors called the flukes the 'hand of God'.

Calves are born into mixed groups and grow up within these family units. Here they play with the other calves of the school (usually their cousins) and may be looked after by several adults in addition to their mothers. The inherent vulnerability of young sperm whale calves could be one of the factors that has favored the evolution of a complex social organization. Calves remain dependent on their mothers for an extended period. They start to take solid food when they are less

'Moby Dick', the white whale in Herman Melville's eponymous novel,
was danger and malevolence personified. This tranquil scene, of a rare pure white
calf and its mother off the Azores, could hardly be more different, a reflection of our changing
perceptions. These magnificent animals now fill us with awe and wonder rather than fear and anger.

Safe below its mother's broad tail this large calf is positioning itself to suckle.

than a year old but they continue to suckle for about five years and some may continue to take milk into their teens.

Exactly how the calf manages to suckle with its long thin jaw is not known, but it is thought that when the mother is at the surface, the calf makes a short dive below her tail and takes the nipple into the angle of the jaw, and the rich milk is expressed into its mouth. One particular problem that sperm whale calves face is that they are unable follow their mothers on deep, feeding dives. Left alone at the surface, young calves are playful and curious and seem oblivious to danger. A calf may join another adult, probably an aunt or uncle, who may stand in as a 'baby-sitter', but on most occasions they are to be found swimming along purposefully, seemingly keeping track of their mothers thousands of feet below, presumably by listening to her clicks. Eventually, her dive over, the mother surfaces again, usually close to the calf, and the two are united until the next dive.

These calves, seemingly abandoned at the surface, may appear vulnerable to predators such as killer whales and sharks. Even if it could alert its mother to the presence of a predator how could she help? She may be at least a mile (0.6 km) below the surface. It is not that sperm whales lack a strong maternal instinct; the old whalers knew that if they caught a sperm whale calf the mother would always stay around and protect it, and cynically they used this as a way of killing both mother and calf. Recently, whale watchers in the Azores observed an adult female carrying a dead calf in her mouth, demonstrating the strength of the bond between mothers and calves.

How can an animal that breeds so slowly and looks after its calves for so long afford to leave them alone at the surface? Simply being within the school may provide enough protection. The calf will normally be surrounded by a 'flotilla' of 20 or so foraging sperm whales, and it has been shown that when there are calves in the group the adults stagger their dives so there is always likely to be one of them near the surface. Perhaps all these vigilant animals create a protective cordon through which predators are unlikely to pass undetected.

Sperm whales exhibit cooperative defensive behaviors when threatened by killer whales or man. Yankee whalers used to say that sperm whales were dangerous at both ends because both their flukes and their jaws were formidable weapons. Sperm whales have been seen to take up defensive formations to exploit both of these. Keeping the most vulnerable members, such as the calves, in the center they form a ring with either their heads or their flukes pointing outwards. The latter is such a characteristic arrangement that it has been dubbed the 'marguerite flower formation'.

Females usually remain within their family groups, and between the ages of 7 and 13 they become sexually mature and start breeding. Calves are born singly after a lengthy gestation period of about 16 months. They have to be cared for for several years and this dictates that calving rates are low, about one every five years. In fact, the reproductive rate of sperm whales is the lowest known for any animal, just one of the factors that makes them so vulnerable to whaling, or any form of mortality.

Young male sperm whales leave their family groups as they reach maturity at around six years of age. They form all-male groups of their own and move into colder, more productive waters where the feeding is better. Although they may be sexually mature when they leave their family groups, they will have to wait many years and put on a lot of bulk before, as prime breeding bulls, they return to the warm waters inhabited by mixed groups. The social organization of males is less well known than that of the females but one piece of evidence that suggests that males are tied by social bonds is that if they strand, they are usually found in groups of 3-10. Male groups seem to be smaller than those of females, they are probably less long-term and are unlikely to be based on family relationships. As the males age they tend to be found in smaller groups and colder waters, but it is only the largest and oldest males which seem to be solitary.

The breeding system is another aspect of sperm whale biology that is poorly understood. We do know that large bulls travel down into warmer waters to join female groups to breed. It had once been assumed that these males were 'harem masters' controlling a social group for long periods of time; some even thought they provided the 'social glue' that held the groups together. In fact, their mating strategy

During periods when they are feeding, members of a social group are typically
seen recovering at the surface singly, or side by side in small groups. The whale on the
right has a dorsal fin callus, a patch of roughened skin that is more common in adult females.

seems to be quite different. They travel between groups searching for receptive females and staying with each group for only a few hours at time.

It is a striking sight to see a large male in a mixed group, they are so much larger, and their heads are so much more prominent. When visiting female groups they announce their presence by producing extremely loud resonant clicks, known as 'clangs'. Most surprising to me was the behavior of the members of mixed groups during these visits. I had expected these huge males to be forcing their attentions on unwilling females; what I observed underwater could not have been more different. The male was the focus of intense attention from all group members, who crowded in on him, rolling themselves along his huge body. They just seemed delighted that he was there. For his part the male was all calm serenity and gentleness. Even the calves were interested and on one occasion we saw a male gently carrying a calf in its mouth.

The sperm whale mating system cannot be entirely without violence, however. The very fact that males have evolved to be so much larger than females suggests that at some stage they compete in ways that favor greater size and strength. Mature males bear long white scars on their heads, rakes from the teeth of other males during some desperate conflicts. However, fights between males have only been seen by whalers, and in situations where whaling may have disturbed the status quo. Males observed on the breeding grounds in recent years appear to avoid or tolerate each other; some even seem to form breeding coalitions. Clearly, there is fierce competition between males, but probably not on the breeding grounds themselves. In fact, very few mature males are actually seen with mixed groups, even at the height of the breeding season. It is also known that some males of breeding age are to be found on feeding grounds, thousands of miles from the females, right through the breeding season. It seems then that males don't attempt to breed every year. There may be some competitive mechanism for determining which males will make the journey to the breeding grounds each year, but what this is, is not known.

This male visiting a social group is the center of attention from all members of the school.

Both males and females live in social units, but what are the benefits that led this trait to evolve? The need for a deep diving animal to care for calves over an extended period seems to be one important factor, but it may not be the whole story, and it does not explain why the males are social. Foraging strategies could provide an additional explanation. Sperm whales have to find elusive prey that are distributed in a huge volume of ocean, and once they have found a school of prey at depth they cannot stay with it for long before they have to return to the surface. When sperm whales are feeding, they are typically spread out in a long rank abreast of each other, anything from hundreds, to thousands of feet apart. Just by listening to the clicks of their fellows they will be able to keep track of where they are and how well they are feeding, sharing information on prey distribution, and thus foraging cooperatively. So, living in groups could greatly enhance their ability to find and exploit food.

Schools, especially the mixed schools and the old matriarchs that may lead them, could also serve as repositories of knowledge. The oceans are constantly changing, both seasonally and over longer, less predictable time periods (the *El Niño* events for example). Knowing where to find food and safety in different situations will mean the difference between life and death. Sperm whales have to stay within good feeding areas, especially if their calves are to survive, and they have the capacity to range over whole ocean basins to find them. The experience of a long-lived animal, especially within a social group, can be used to guide the entire group to the best areas when conditions change. A long-term social group provides a mechanism for that knowledge to continue beyond the lifetime of any one individual.

We are only just beginning to scratch the surface as far as knowledge of sperm whale social behavior is concerned. What is clear already is that being social is central to the species' survival strategy; to understand sperm whales we have to understand their social organization, and to protect and conserve them, we must ensure that their social organization remains intact.

Tooth marks, probably from killer whales, indicate that this whale has been attacked.

The World's Most Impressive Diver

Sperm whales make their impressive dives continuously. Every day of its life, and every hour of the day and night, a sperm whale makes an amazing vertical journey into a deep-water realm. It has become something of a cliché, but it is none the less true, to say that we know more about the surface of the moon than we do about the deep oceans. It is also about as difficult for people to get there. Undeterred, the sperm whale makes regular passages between the deep cold depths and the sunlit waters of the surface. The sperm whale is the world's greatest breath-hold diver, making dives that can last well over an hour and may take it over 6560 ft (2000 m) deep. Most of a sperm whale's daily life is spent in bouts of long, deep, feeding dives and during these, its behavior can become extremely predictable. It spends about ten minutes at the surface between each dive, breathing strongly and steadily. Then, taking one last gulp of air, it raises its flukes gracefully above the surface to initiate a vertical dive, disappearing from view with barely a splash.

Our knowledge of sperm whale behavior during these deep dives is extremely sparse, pulled together from a variety of disparate sources. The fact that sperm whales have been discovered entangled in deep-sea telegraph cables indicates that they can descend to at least 7220 ft (2200 m), while sonar observations from a submarine show that they can reach 8200 ft (2500 m). Various observations with sonar and depth sounders suggest that a typical dive consists of a near-vertical initial phase, leveling off beyond 1640 ft (500 m) where foraging may take place. A small amount of more detailed data has come from tagged animals, while analyzing the whales' vocalizations during their dives provides further tantalizing insights into their underwater behavior. We do at least know what motivates sperm whales to make these impressive dives. The stomachs of sperm whales yield the remains of many deep-sea squid and fish; in fact, in the times of whaling, sperm whale stomachs were

The fluke-up is the graceful movement that marks the beginning of the whale's vertical journey.

often the only source for specimens of many of these mysterious deep-sea species. We are a long way from understanding precisely what sperm whales do on these dives, how they manage to feed and what physiological adaptations allow them to perform these feats, but to gain some appreciation of what the underwater world of the sperm whale might be like, let us imagine following a sperm whale on one typical dive.

Our whale has been up on the surface for about ten minutes, blowing strongly every 12 seconds or so through its single blowhole, each exhalation a small explosion of vapor, each inhalation a rapid intake of breath. Whales' lungs are proportionately smaller than our own; they are very efficient at exchanging gas, for, during this brief period at the surface, they must in effect do all the breathing for the next 45 minutes of active underwater swimming. A sperm whale at the surface usually moves slowly and predictably, its whole reason for being there is to rid its body of carbon dioxide and load it up with oxygen. In whales, the main oxygen store is in the muscles, where a molecule called myoglobin binds and holds it until required. Different muscles in different animals have differing amounts of myoglobin in them. A chicken's breast muscles, for example, which have no capacity for long-term exertion, are white because they contain little myoglobin. Its leg muscles, which are constantly active, have more myoglobin and are much darker.

Swimming slowly in a rank, as seen from the air.

Three whales make a shallow dive in synchrony.

*Raising its flukes high in the air, a whale begins its dive into a dark, cold,
deep-water realm that is still rarely visited by man. The most impressive of mammalian divers,
sperm whales may reach depths in excess of 6560 ft (2000 m) and remain submerged for over an hour.*

The flesh of the sperm whale contains so much myoglobin it looks like congealed blood and is almost black in color. Once it has replenished its oxygen supplies our whale takes two more forceful breaths and, rounding its body up, brings its flukes gracefully above the water to initiate its vertical dive. It vanishes from sight, with hardly a splash, leaving a spreading circular slick of smooth water on the surface.

Each powerful beat of the whale's flukes takes it deeper, away from the surface sunshine and into the cold, dark depths. The whale is swimming at about 3½ miles per hour (5.6 kpm), a brisk walking pace. This is not the fastest it can swim but it is close to being its most efficient speed. What the whale needs to do is maximize the amount of oxygen it has left to forage with when it reaches its feeding depths. If it swims too quickly it will burn it all up; if it swims too slowly it will run out of time.

As soon as the whale leaves the surface, physiological mechanisms come into play, to manage the use of its precious oxygen supply while making sure that the vital organs and the brain are always kept supplied. The heart rate drops dramatically, and blood supply to peripheral regions and non-essential processes, such as digestion, are curtailed.

About three minutes into the dive the whale has reached 820 ft (250 m). It has already exceeded the depths at which a human diver breathing air can work. The air the whale dived with is 25 per cent of its volume, and its lungs and jointed rib cage have collapsed. The air has become a precious resource to be saved and recycled in sound production, or spread thinly within air spaces so they will still reflect sound and function as sound mirrors (see page 49).

Light is reduced to a twilight glimmer and now the whale starts clicking. The first few clicks are tentative, but the whale is soon into a steady rhythm of about one click per second. Each click is like a small detonation, spreading out into the surrounding medium and bouncing back from objects in its path. The whale listens to these echoes, its main clues for navigating and finding its prey. The strongest echoes come back first from the sea surface, far above it, and from the sea floor, far below. It makes its next click after it receives the bottom echo. Synchronizing its clicks to these returning echoes the whale swims on, and as it gets closer to the bottom, still over 3280 ft (1000 m) away, its rate of clicking slowly increases.

The whale swims steadily on to a depth of 1640 ft (500 m). This is the absolute limit at which humans can work and they can only manage this by using exotic mixtures of gases. The process of getting there and returning to the surface involves days of compression and decompression in a special chamber. At this depth it is almost completely dark. Something in the returning echoes catches its interest and the whale diverts slightly to investigate. As it approaches it clicks faster and faster until its trains of clicks sound like a creaking door. A sizeable deep-sea shark is snapped up and vanishes.

Between 1640 and 3280 ft (500 and 1000 m) our whale is in its main hunting grounds. It is dark, cold, and timeless, pitch black day and night and a constant 2°C winter and summer. Virtually no light penetrates from the surface, but it is not completely dark; many deep-sea animals are bioluminescent and when disturbed they sparkle and glow. This is also the depth of the deep sound channel, a sound duct that traps and funnels sounds, allowing low-frequency sound to propagate immense distances. The whale's sensitive ears pick up a great panorama of sounds, remote shipping, earthquakes, a distant storm, but usually dominating it all are the clicks of its school-mates, spread out feeding over an area of tens of square miles and, like him, probing the oceans with sound. Listening to the patterns of its companions' clicks and creaks the whale can hear how well they are feeding, and equally its own vocalizations tell of its own success. In this way, without any need for a structured language or special signs, information on feeding conditions over a vast area spreads instantly through the school.

Now our whale is hunting in earnest, but exactly how a sperm whale accomplishes this most fundamental of activities remains one of its best-kept secrets. Needless to say, no one has ever seen a sperm whale feed and there are

Three whales seem almost to be dancing as they roll together underwater.

All the main features of the whale can be seen in this fully developed calf.
Note its eye on a slightly protruding part of the body and its long, thin white-coloured jaw.

some fundamental problems to explain. In these deep waters there is no light from the surface; no problem, you might think, sperm whales echolocate. They do, but squid, their main food, contain no air-filled or hard structures, and thus do not reflect sound at all well. Underwater, sound literally passes straight though them, making them difficult targets to find in the great three-dimensional vastness of the deep ocean. By dint of its huge size, the sperm whale has enormous inertia and poor acceleration. By contrast its main prey, the jet-propelled squid, are swift and maneuverable, the masters of the quick getaway. It has been calculated that by the time a sperm whale had accelerated its bulk to the speed of a squid it would have used up more energy than it could get by digesting the prey, even if it caught it.

Although sperm whales do occasionally capture large prey, even the giant squid *Architeuthis* itself, the majority of its diet is made up of small, luminous, neutrally buoyant squid, too small to be captured individually. Wherever facts are sparse theories abound; and there has been no shortage of new ideas over the years to explain sperm whale feeding.

Thomas Beale, a surgeon on a British sperm whaler, summarized the views of the early whalers. Quite sensibly, they believed that the lower jaw might act as a giant squid lure. Its white coloration and ivory teeth (in the males at least) might make it even more attractive in the bioluminescent glow from squid or other animals. Feeding squid seem inclined to grab hold of anything remotely interesting, as the success of squid jigging as a fishing technique testifies. Once attached, a quick snap of the narrow jaw should be enough to kill or disable them so that they could be scooped into its mouth by the whale's long thin tongue.

A more recent embellishment of this idea is the proposal that the jaw might become smeared with the bioluminescent slime from squid, making it an even more effective lure. Others have their own explanations. Perhaps the very loud clicks that sperm whales make underwater could stun their prey, making them easy to catch. There are now observations of killer whales using shock-waves to stun herring at the surface, but squid seem incredibly resistant to being stunned underwater. Perhaps, though, a sonic shock-wave could make bioluminescent animals light up, illuminating any squid nearby, just as the disturbance of a ship at the surface causes phosphorescence in its wake. Often, sperm whales are hunting within the water depths with the lowest levels of dissolved oxygen in the whole water column. In some oceans this 'oxygen minimum layer' can be virtually anoxic. Obviously, such low levels of dissolved oxygen will greatly reduce the capacity of any animal that obtains its oxygen from the water (including all deep-water fish and squid) to be active. A diving

mammal, that brings its own oxygen stores down with it from the surface, suffers no such constraint and is at a tremendous advantage. One might imagine an active sperm whale feeding on schools of comatose squid and fish. However it manages to do it, we do know that sperm whales are very successful feeders in these deep waters. A moderate-sized sperm whale would have to catch around 1100 lb (500 kg) of food per day which could represent as many as 1000 squid.

The oceanic sperm whale rarely comes this close to land.

We left our sperm whale feeding at a depth of around 3280 ft (1000 m). This is by no means the limit of its range; sperm whales have been recorded at least twice as deep as this, but let us consider for a while the physical and physiological problems that our whale has had to overcome to perform this (for him) mundane dive. At 3280 ft (1000 m) the air that the whale dived with has been reduced to one per cent of its original volume. Its lungs are squashed flat and the air is probably confined to the nasal passages, a precious commodity to be carefully distributed amongst air spaces to enable them to reflect sound, and recycled through the sound producing organs to produce clicks. If the air is one per cent of

A sperm whale fluke-up is a moment of great beauty. The flexible flukes hang
down from the wrist-like joint at the end of the tail as an unbroken waterfall streams from them.

the volume, it is also 100 times its density and thus more viscous, physically quite different from the gases we are used to. When a human dives the most obvious effect of the increased pressure of the water is the necessity to equalize pressure in the ears and the head sinuses. If this is not done carefully it is incredibly painful and can even lead to ruptured eardrums or sinus membranes. Whales have dispensed with the complex sinuses in the head and they have wide straight eustachian tubes to their ears so that pressure can be equalized readily. A human diver holding his breath would soon become aware of pressure on his chest, and if forced to dive too deep his ribs would eventually break. Whales' ribs are adapted to fold up so that the lungs can squash completely flat.

One serious problem for human scuba divers, decompression sickness or the 'bends', comes when they attempt to return to the surface too quickly after a long dive. While a scuba diver is at depth, the tissues of his body become saturated with gas at the elevated pressure at which he has been working. It can take a long time for this gas to be removed, especially from tissues like muscles, tendons and bone. Come up too fast and the effect is akin to taking the lid off a pop-bottle. Free gas comes out of solution within the body with potentially lethal consequences. To overcome this, human divers have to make decompression stops and come to the surface slowly enough to allow the gas to equilibrate. It can take days to bring a diver back from deep saturation dives. How then can sperm whales pop up and down to much deeper depths, seemingly as fast as they please? In the first place sperm whales are breath-hold divers, so they do not breathe compressed air. Therefore there is a much-reduced potential for their bodies to become saturated. Even so, because they spend such a large proportion of their lives at such great depths, their bodies should become supersaturated with gas. They probably avoid absorbing compressed gas during dives by allowing it to be squashed out of their lungs and into the much

How sweet the first breath of air must be after an hour-long dive.

less absorptive passageways of the larynx and nasal passages, but in addition, it seems from studies with dolphins, that these diving animals have some special resistance to developing the 'bends'.

The effects of these immense pressures go well beyond their simple physical effects on gases; they can affect fundamental biochemical processes as well. In human divers, for example, compression of the junctions in the nervous pathways to the muscles causes them to fire spontaneously and leads to uncontrolled shaking, so-called 'deep pressure nervous syndrome'. Elevated pressure can also cause cell microtubules to break down, making such fundamental processes as cell division impossible. Of course, all deep-sea vertebrates have had to solve these effects of pressure, what is unique about sperm whales is their ability to function in such a wide and rapidly changing range of pressures. Each increase in the depth limit for human divers seems to reveal new and unexpected biochemical and physiological effects of pressure; sperm whales may well have overcome obstacles whose existence we don't even suspect.

Forty minutes into the dive and the whale senses that it is time to return to the surface. Probably it could stay down even longer, but only by using wasteful metabolic processes and running up a so-called 'oxygen debt' that will mean a much longer period of recovery at the surface. With the same steady unhurried strokes our whale heads through the black waters, up towards the surface. Almost imperceptibly, but unmistakably, it is getting lighter, and the surface can be seen as a distant glow far ahead. The whale has been making long sequences of clicks almost continuously while underwater, but now these become erratic and cease. At last the surface comes into sight, shafts of sunlight and a strange landscape made by the underside of the breaking waves. Finally its blowhole reaches the surface and it exhales, sending up a puff of vapor and, almost an hour since it last did so, it fills its lungs. How sweet that first breath of salty air must be.

Their buoyancy perfectly balanced, a mother and full-grown calf loll together in mid-water.

The Acoustic World of the Sperm Whale

Sperm whales are highly vocal animals, emitting loud, regular clicks almost continuously while they are underwater. They have sensitive hearing and a well-developed echolocation system. Most impressively of all they have given over as much as 33 per cent of their body length to their head, the world's biggest natural sound-producing mechanism. This staggering degree of acoustic specialization is explained by one inescapable physical fact: sound propagates through the oceans more efficiently than any other form of energy. In fact, it propagates far more efficiently through water than it does through air, five times faster.

I have to admit that on first acquaintance, sperm whale vocalizations can seem rather monotonous. Humpback whales make beautiful long songs; dolphins produce a wide variety of different whistles but sperm whales just click, usually very regularly, at a rate of about 2 per second, on and on and on. A school of sperm whales clicking in the distance sounds like a herd of 'sound effect' horses at full gallop. So loud are their clicks that in the days of sail, seamen would hear them through the hulls of their vessels, and likening the noise to nails being banged home, called them the 'carpenter fish'.

The main function of a sperm whale's click is echolocation. An echolocating animal makes a loud noise then listens for echoes returning from reflective objects. It obtains information about the type and location of objects in its environment from the time it takes the echo to return (which gives range), the direction it comes from (which gives bearing) and qualitative features of the echo (which may tell it the size, shape and texture). Sequences of clicks are interspersed with silences and bursts of very rapid clicking or 'creaks'. Creaks are almost identical to the buzzes that dolphins make as they close in on their prey, and it seems likely that sperm whale creaks represent feeding attempts as well.

Sperm whale clicks do not seem to be very directional, in this sense they are

Members of a social group observed from the air at the surface off Dominica.

unlike the echolocation clicks of many dolphins which are produced in a directional beam, a bit like an acoustic searchlight. If a sperm whale investigates an object at the surface, a boat or a swimmer for example, then it also emits sequences of rapid clicks in a directional beam. These seem to be much like creaks and it is likely that creaks are directional too. It seems then, that sperm whales have two modes of echolocation. The slow, regular, non-directional clicks are an omni-directional, low acuity, long-range echolocation system, for navigation and finding large objects, in the vast three-dimensional spaces through which the whale hunts for its food. The rapid, directional click trains, such as creaks, are high acuity, short-range, beamed echolocation more akin to that used by dolphins and bats.

Sperm whales also communicate using their clicks. At the most basic level, being able to hear other whales clicking at ranges of several miles must serve to keep the school together, and possibly also to spread information through the school on the availability of food. Sperm whales also make clicks in characteristic, stereotyped patterns, called codas, and these seem to be adapted for direct communication. Codas are heard most frequently during periods when whales come together in large groups to rest and socialize at the surface. Codas vary in both the number of clicks and in their pattern. We might think of them as a form of Morse code. If codas do represent a very simple 'language' we are a long way from understanding it. Some studies have given fascinating insights; for example, the structure of codas seems to follow certain rules. The interval between clicks in a coda is either normal, or long (approximately twice the normal interval). Some codas seem to be particularly popular but these frequent-use codas vary from population to population. In the Galapagos, for example, 'five-click' codas (///// or //// /) are used most frequently, in the Azores it is five regular (/ / / / /), in the Caribbean it is two long intervals followed by three faster ones (/ / ///) while around Sri Lanka (// /). Intriguingly, in the Mediterranean only one coda type (/// /) has ever been recorded.

Codas often take the form of exchanges between whales in a group. Sometimes whales respond with the same coda, sometimes with a different one.

A whale blows as its blowhole is still breaking the surface.
Note the characteristic low bushy blow deflected to the left.

A sperm whale eyes the photographer it has just swum past in clear, sunlit,
surface waters off the Azores. In these conditions, vision is important, in deep waters when
visibility is poor acoustics become the most important sense. The paddle-shaped fins are shown
well in this picture. The five bones that correspond to fingers can be distinguished as slight protuberances.

Research in the Galapagos indicated that these exchanges may be structured. Some codas, the 'five-click' coda for example, tended to initiate exchanges, while 'eight-click' codas often came before 'seven-click' codas, but rarely the other way round.

It seems then that sperm whales may have a sophisticated form of vocal communication and that the information is contained in the number and pattern of the clicks. Most other mammals communicate by varying the pitch of their calls, so why do sperm whales use such an unusual pattern-based system? The reverberant oceanic environment in which sperm whales communicate can distort acoustic signals so that their meaning is lost. Codas resemble a simple form of digital communication and will be less susceptible to distortion, suiting them for exchanging information over long distances in a difficult environment.

The most impressive sounds that sperm whales make are the extremely loud 'clangs' that often announce the presence of mature males visiting females in a social group. These powerful, resonant clicks are made in very slow sequences, about one every five seconds. They 'sound' so powerful it seems probable that they are some form of display, either to impress the females or warn off other males.

Clicks are produced in the sperm whale's enormous head. This huge structure is made up of two large fat-filled bodies, the 'spermaceti sac' and the 'junk' and it also contains a network of air filled passages. The left nasal passage is a broad straight tube used for breathing, and it runs directly from the blowhole to the lungs. The right nasal passage connects to the left nasal tube just below the blowhole and passes back to the lungs too, but on the way it meanders, becomes flattened and in places extends into pockets to create a number of air sacs. Even a thin film of air acts as an excellent reflector of sound underwater and these sacs are thought to function as 'sound mirrors' in the whale's body. Most important of these are the frontal sac that extends over the parabola-shaped front of the skull, and a distal sac at the very front of the head. Just behind the distal sac the right nasal tube passes through a strong valve that looks like a pair of monkey lips (hence its name, *museau de singe*). This is thought to be the source of the clicks.

The spermaceti organ is a long sac, filled with the special spermaceti oil from which this whale gets its name. Spermaceti has always been a prized substance, first as the source of the very finest wax for smokeless candles, and later, until alternatives were developed, as a fine grade engineering lubricant used in everything from watches to rocket motors.

Below the spermaceti organ is a second large fatty organ, the 'junk'. Whalers gave it this dismissive name because it was of less commercial value than the spermaceti. This unflattering name seems to have colored the perceptions of scientists too, for its function in sound production has received much less attention than that of the spermaceti sac, even though its structure, being made up of a stack of lens-shaped fat bodies, is very exciting, and suggests that it has an important role.

It seems probable that sperm whales might assess each other's size acoustically. We know that males fight with each other, it is in the course of these fights that they pick up the striking tooth rakes on their bodies. Usually, in nature, adversaries in conflicts assess each other carefully before they allow fights to escalate. Put simply, they don't want to risk getting badly hurt in a fight if they don't think they have a good chance of winning it. It would be difficult for a whale to visually assess the size of an adversary underwater because visual range is so limited, but the unique pulsed nature of sperm whale clicks may allow them to do this acoustically. The heads of male sperm whales are proportionally larger than those of females and acoustic size estimation might explain why this is so. Whales which developed longer heads would 'sound' even larger than they actually were, they would thus be better able to intimidate opponents and so gain a competitive advantage. Females don't fight to the same extent as males and an ability to 'sound big' would not have such a great adaptive advantage for them. Thus, evolution would result in proportionally larger heads in males. Understanding the central role of acoustics in the life of sperm whales is crucial to appreciating the true nature of the animal.

The great bulk of a sperm whale's head obscures its vision directly forward

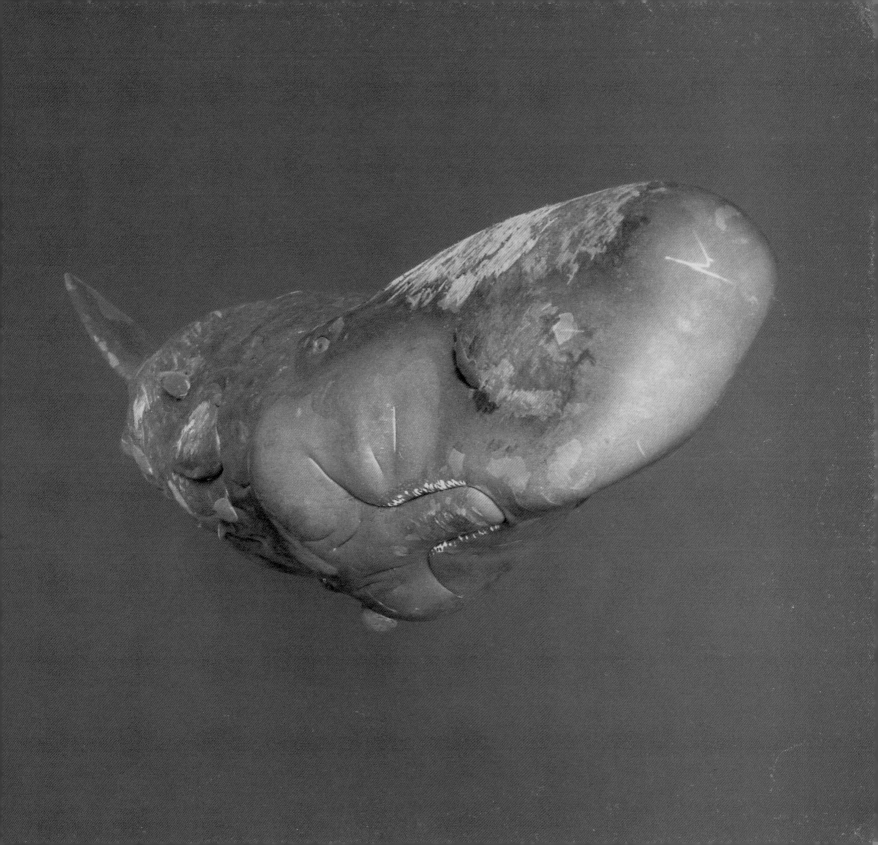

A sperm whale fluking up is not just a beautiful natural spectacle. Photographs of the trailing edge can be used by scientists like a finger print to identify individual whales.

Benign Research

In the still, gray light of a breaking dawn, under the towering bulk of Pico, an extinct volcano in the Azores, a small sailing boat is motoring steadily towards a small silver puff that appears intermittently, highlighted against the dull-gray water. These puffs are the blows of a sperm whale recovering at the surface after a long, deep dive. The boat describes a wide slow arc, so that it approaches the whale from directly behind, and, as it gets close, slows until it barely has steerage-way. There are two people in the boat's cockpit; one of them picks up a camera with a long lens, and stumbles along to the foredeck. In the colorless light everything is gray. The whale, a darker gray mass lies about 100 ft (33 m) ahead, just awash in the slight swell. Eventually, the whale is ready to dive again, and its steady rhythm of blows changes. It takes a few deeper breaths, raising its head higher in the water and flexing its body, before rounding up and bringing its flukes above the water to begin its dive.

As the flukes are raised vertically there is a fusillade from the camera as a sequence of photographs are taken, by the time the photographer looks up from the eyepiece the whale has gone. He moves back to the cockpit, picks up a form and writes down some information about the encounter that has just ended, and the pictures he has taken. Other information on the boat's locations is being logged continuously on a computer linked to the boat's satellite Global Positioning System (GPS). When the photographs are processed the research team will be able to examine the flukes and identify the whale. Putting this information together with all the other pieces of data collected on hundreds of such encounters, through the seasons and over the years, will build up a detailed picture of the behavior of these whales and their social organization. The whale they have just seen is by now hundreds of feet down, swimming inexorably on towards the bottom. The team have been up for the last four hours tracking these whales through the night using hydrophones, but it looks set to be a long exciting day with sperm whales.

Because they live so far offshore, and disappear from the surface for long periods of time on their deep dives, sperm whales have always been considered one of the most difficult of animals to investigate. The whole concept of studying the behavior of live whales is a fairly recent one. Initially, research started on whales that could be easily observed from the shore, such as gray whales and southern right whales, it then moved on to other species such as humpbacks, in regions where they come close to land. Studying live sperm whales in the open ocean required the development of a new approach and this grew out of the World Wide Fund for Nature (WWF) 'Tulip' project lead by Hal Whitehead in the Indian Ocean Whale Sanctuary in the early 1980s. The two key elements to this way of working are the use of small offshore sailing vessels as research platforms so that teams can spend long periods working safely and independently at sea; and employing passive acoustics as a means of finding sperm whales and tracking them while they dive.

The boat we have been watching, one early morning off the Azores, is *Song of the Whale*, a 46 ft (14 m) ketch that I run as a research boat for the International Fund for Animal Welfare. It is one of only a few boats world-wide that has been specially equipped to study live sperm whales offshore, and what better way to find out how we go about this than to follow her through a typical day of research work.

In the first place, how was it that the boat came to be so conveniently positioned within a short distance of whales at first light? The answer, of course, is that the crew had been following whales, by listening to their clicks, through the night. Sperm whales are virtually never seen from *Song of the Whale* without being heard first. No sooner had the boat left harbor on a research cruise the previous evening, than the main towed hydrophone was streamed astern of the boat on a 330 ft- (100 m-) long cable. The hydrophone itself consists of two sensitive elements (a bit like microphones) in a 33-ft (10-m) long, oil-filled polythene tube. Being in a long flexible tube reduces water noise so that the hydrophone can be listened to while the boat is underway. This vital piece of equipment is really as simple as it

With its buoyancy perfectly adjusted, this whale is equally at home 'upside down' as right way up.

When sperm whales are resting and socialising, researchers
can slip into the water and collect pieces of skin that naturally sloughs from
the animals and floats free in the water. This swimmer has mistakenly got too close. Such
close encounters, that could both disturb the whales and endanger the swimmer, are not encouraged.

sounds, and the team usually make their own. As the rest of the crew settled down for the night the pair on watch continued their vigil. The hydrophone was monitored carefully every 15 minutes through the night and all the data describing what was heard when and where was entered into a computer. On most stations, they could hear dolphins whistling or clicking. When they happened to listen close to a dolphin school their vocalizations drowned everything else out completely. There were other noises too, often the rumble of distant shipping, rarely absent in the world's oceans these days. You can hear ships clearly even when there is nothing to be seen to the horizon. Then, there is the sound of the sea itself, as it gets rougher, levels of background noise from things like breaking waves increase markedly, but on this still night it was just a gentle murmur. Over the years, all this acoustic monitoring information is being compiled to produce detailed offshore distribution maps.

When the first faint clicks of sperm whales were eventually detected, the boat was stopped and a directional hydrophone lowered from the stern. By rotating this while listening to it, a bearing on the whales can be obtained and the boat heads off in that direction. Luckily, it was a calm night and the crew, working on the moonlit aft deck, could get a very precise bearing on the whales. The towed hydrophone provides directional information too. There are two hydrophones in the array, and by listening to these in stereo you can determine which of the two hydrophone elements the clicks are striking first, and thus whether the whale is in front or behind. Whales are normally detected at ranges of about 5 miles (8 km) and it takes a few stops with the directional hydrophone and a change of watch before the boat is right on top of the group.

At first light the whales are there and a long day spent moving between whales in the group gets underway. Often the most important information to collect from whales while they are recovering from dives is photographic. Sperm whales may look like smooth featureless logs at the surface, but closer examination reveals small patches of rough skin – calluses – on their dorsal fins. These are more common on mature females and so can provide a reasonable indication of some animals' age and sex. Photographs taken from up the mast in the crow's nest, which show the whale's back and the horizon, can be analyzed to measure sperm whales' length, while photographs of the whales' tails, taken as the whale flukes up before deep dives, allow most of the whales to be identified as individuals. Being able to identify individual whales in this way allows many different aspects of their biology, such as their movements and migrations, to be investigated, but most importantly for sperm whales, it provides a new insight into their social organization. Thousands of sperm whales have been identified by different research groups in the Atlantic and the Pacific; by organizing their photographs into catalogs and exchanging these they can share information on the whales' social organization and movements.

Soon after whales fluke up, they start clicking and then very clear recordings of the clicks of identified whales can be made which can be analyzed to measure the inter-pulse intervals allowing an acoustic determination of body length to be made. It is also possible to track the whale's dives using a simple depth sounder so that, during the initial stage of a dive, good data on descent rates can be obtained.

With so much data to collect, the boat is a hive of activity. Everyone has a specific job and these change on a rota every few hours. One person is always at the wheel, responsible for steering the boat. Maneuvering carefully around whales without disturbing them is quite a skill and an experienced team member is always on hand to make sure it is done properly. Another person is on watch in the crow's nest some 33 ft (10 m) above the deck. They are in the best place to spot whales and guide the helmsman to them; they also take length-measuring pictures when the boat gets close enough. Another one or two people are responsible for taking identification photographs of flukes and dorsal fins during encounters. Somehow everything must be written down on the right piece of paper or entered into the correct computer table. The most important, but least favored, task is that of achieving this, keeping track and recording all the data while the boat responds to each new sighting.

Resting whales swim slowly in typical formation, close together and in line abreast.

It is fiercely hot by midday and the azure ocean that surrounds the team looks increasingly enticing. The whales' pattern of behavior seems to be changing though. They are spending longer on the surface and are moving together into larger groups. The cacophony of click trains on the hydrophones is subsiding and being replaced by occasional stereotyped patterns of clicks (codas, see page 46). Within an hour there are no whales making deep dives and *Song of the Whale* is hove-to about 1640 ft (500 m) from a group of at least 12 whales. For some periods, the whales seem totally inactive, breathing infrequently and shallowly with hardly a blow. Then they may become livelier, showing their heads and the side of their flukes above the water as they roll against each other and interact at the surface. Some few hundred feet from the main group, a whale is lobtailing.

A little later a whale flukes up some way from the group; everyone who can grabs a camera and trains it hopefully towards the slick. Often a fluke up during a resting period precedes a breach, surely one of the most spectacular displays in the animal kingdom. Suddenly the still ocean erupts as, like a Polaris missile, a sperm whale bursts through its surface. The whale rises almost to its full height slowing as gravity takes hold of over ten tons of whale flesh. The whale seems to hover, seemingly defying gravity for a moment, before toppling sideways and returning to the water with a crash. A tower of white water rises high into the air as the seas, rushing back in to fill the substantial hole that the whale has just punched in it, collide. The same whale continues with a series of 15 breaches, but each one a bit weaker than the last, until finally it is barely raising its head above the water and it resumes resting at the surface.

For most of this resting period *Song of the Whale* sails slowly some 1640 ft (500 m) from the group, content to hang off and observe from a distance while making recordings of their fascinating patterned coda vocalizations. Because the whales seem very relaxed and move very slowly during these periods, it is an

A sperm whale's head thrusts clear of the water during a gentle breach off the Azores.

occasion when, taking great care, underwater observations can be made. Some unique samples can be collected at the same time. As the whales in the group rub against each other, pieces of their skin are rubbed off and swimmers can snorkel down with hand-nets and collect them. These prove to be ideal samples for DNA fingerprinting analysis, enabling individual whales to be identified and their family relationships investigated. Perhaps this is the most remarkable of any of the benign techniques the boat uses. Once it would have been thought necessary to kill a whale to get a DNA sample, now we know that we can obtain one without the animal even realizing it has 'given' one.

Underwater glimpses of whale social groups are brief but always informative, and they underline how much is missed from the surface. The observers from the boat can see only a few shining backs but underwater the whales are stacked three deep and constantly touching, interacting, rolling their bodies against each other. Glimpses like this emphasize just how deeply social these animals are. They are remarkably well balanced and graceful and seem just as happy floating or swimming in any attitude, upside down, vertically with their heads up or down, it makes no difference. As one whale rolls along the back of a comrade, sheets of skin are dislodged and float off into the water to be left behind in the wake of the slowly moving group. Team members scoop the skin into their nets and take it back to the boat, where it is packed in specimen bottles with salt; at the end of the season it will be sent off to a genetics lab to be analyzed.

This method of collecting skin samples, which also provides glimpses of whales underwater, is a sought-after privilege, and there is no shortage of volunteers. Swimming with whales is not taken lightly on the boat, however. If it is not done carefully there is a real chance of frightening the animals and there are also risks to the swimmers. Any open-ocean swimming is dangerous. The whales themselves always seem completely benign but they are, after all, wild animals and when a creature as puny as a human is in the water with an animal as powerful as a whale there is a risk of being injured, however inadvertently. Certainly, the practice, that is

The sun sets but this makes little difference to a sperm whale that feeds at depths to which little light penetrates. Whales continue to make their deep dives day and night.

Away from the surface, a group of sperm whales move together in a world of three-dimensional space.

growing around the world, of encouraging tourists to swim with sperm whales threatens both the whales and the humans involved and is not to be encouraged.

After a few hours of resting the group seems be getting restless, more animals start to fluke-up and dive and regular feeding clicks are heard on the hydrophones. Eventually, there is only a mother and calf left at the surface where the large group had once been and *Song of the Whale* returns to 'chasing flukes'. They are still there as the sun sets, the scarlet sky and golden light reflecting off the flukes, giving some of the identification photographs an aesthetic appeal to add to their scientific value. It has been a hard but productive and rewarding day and most of the crew would like to pack up and go to bed, but they can't; on *Song of the Whale* it is just the beginning of the night shift. While one of the team makes supper, others try to put order into the plethora of films and data sheets that have resulted from the day's work. Out on deck, the two on watch are already busily tracking the clicks of the whales into another night.

Threats and Conservation

Sperm whales are widely distributed in offshore waters of the world's oceans and have a substantial total population. As such, they can not be considered an acutely endangered species, but history has shown they are unable to withstand direct exploitation, such as whaling and they also seem vulnerable to modern day threats.

For all their simple, un-mechanized tools and haphazard organization, the open-boat whalers of the Yankee era had a devastating effect on sperm whale populations. The records show how, as each new whaling ground was discovered, it would give good catches for a few years before becoming exhausted. It is likely that by the time 'Yankee Whaling' ceased at the beginning of the twentieth century, sperm whale populations were a quarter of their pristine levels. Probably this whaling was particularly destructive because it focused on the females and young in temperate and tropical waters, possibly also disrupting their social organization. Mechanized whaling, later in the century, was directed mainly towards the more profitable large males. These became so depleted however, that by the time sperm whaling finished in the late 1980s it was feared that there were insufficient mature males for effective breeding. The sperm whale's extremely low reproductive rate means that they have a maximum potential rate of increase of less than 1 per cent per annum. They are an animal whose biology simply precludes any rational form of consumptive exploitation.

Sperm whales' offshore distribution had, in the past, kept them away from man's activities in coastal waters. Increasingly though, humans are beginning to exploit the deep-water habitats in which sperm whales live. Deep sea fishes are now targeted by a new generation of trawlers. An activity more akin to mining than harvesting. In surface oceanic waters, drift nets are used and sperm whales appear to be the most vulnerable of any of the great whales to becoming entangled in these and drowning. Sperm whales also seem particularly prone to being hit by shipping, perhaps while they are recovering at the surface between dives. A collision with a large ship can be fatal for a whale. Being at the pinnacle of a long food chain, within which bio-accumulation takes place, sperm whales can accumulate very high levels of pollutants in their bodies. When sperm whales stranded on a Belgian beach recently, their bodies were judged to carry such a high pollutant load that they were classified as toxic waste.

Sperm whales' reliance on sound makes them particularly vulnerable to acoustic disturbance and interference, so called acoustic pollution. A growing number of powerful new sounds in the ocean are giving cause for concern, including those associated with oceanographic experiments, new low frequency military sonar and seismic surveys conducted by the oil industry. Though we still do not understand all the different ways in which sperm whales might use sound in their daily lives, it is clear that sound is their most important sensory modality, and this alone is cause for considerable concern.

The mighty sperm whale, the world's greatest predator, might seem well able to look after itself. In fact, these animals are terribly vulnerable. The deep ocean is no longer a safe refuge from man and their biology makes them susceptible to many of the insults that humans throw at nature in the modern world.

A sperm whale raises its flukes high in the air as it begins its vertical descent on a deep dive off New Zealand.

Where to See Sperm Whales

Being creatures of the open ocean, and deep divers, sperm whales are not the easiest of animals to get to see. Whale watching has developed rather later with sperm whales than it has with some of the more accessible species such as baleen whales and orcas. However, successful sperm whale watching ventures have now sprung up in several different areas. Most are in regions where very deep water can be found close to the shore, underwater canyons and volcanic islands for example.

The most successful sperm whale watching enterprise is off the Kaikoura peninsula in the South Island of New Zealand. This is a feeding area for male sperm whales and whale watching takes place from a fleet of fast inflatable vessels. The whale watching here is run entirely by the local Maori people, continuing a long tradition of cultural involvement with sperm whales.

In the Azores, long the last bastion of traditional Yankee-style whaling, a number of whale watching enterprises have started in recent years. Here both mixed groups and males can be seen and both fast inflatable boats and larger sailing vessels are used. Some trips leave from ex-whaling villages and many of these villages have reinstated the old whaling lookouts or 'vigias' in their special huts in the hills. These are always worth a visit. Here you can get your first sight of sperm whales many miles away, using powerful binoculars on solid land.

Andenes, in northern Norway, is another prime sperm whale watching location where large males can be seen from converted fishing boats. A number of Caribbean Islands, notably the Commonwealth of Dominica, are also establishing whale watching operations.

Several aspects of sperm whales, including their sensitivity to sound, their reliance on social structures and low reproductive rate make them particularly vulnerable to disturbance. It is thus important that whale watching operators behave sensitively with sperm whales and adhere to appropriate codes of conduct.

A calf at ease with its mother in gin-clear, sun-suffused waters at the ocean surface. Man is increasingly exploiting these same waters however, and sperm whales face a number of new threats in the modern world.

Sperm Whale Facts

Common Name	Sperm Whale	
Scientific Name	*Physeter macrocephalus*	
Body Measurements	Female	Male
Length at Birth	13 ft (4 m)	13 ft (4 m)
Weight at Birth	c 1 tonne	c 1 tonne
Length at Sexual Maturity	28½ ft (8.7 m)	39½ ft (12 m)
Age at Sexual Maturity	9	19
Length at Physical Maturity	35¾ ft (10.9 m)	52 ft (15.9 m)
Weight at Physical Maturity	13.5 tonnes	43.6 tonnes
Age at Sexual Maturity	45	30
Duration of Gestation	16 months	
Duration of Lactation	5 years	
Calving Interval	5 years	

Distribution: Sperm whales are usually confined to deep waters >1640 ft (500 m), however they are found throughout most of the world's oceans. Females and young stay in tropical and temperate waters, approximately between 40°S and 40°N and only mature males venture into colder waters.

Biographical Note

Dr Jonathan Gordon is a zoologist, based in the Wildlife Conservation Research Unit of Oxford University Zoology Department and runs a 46 ft (14 m) 'ketch'. *Song of the Whale* is a research boat for the International Fund for Animal Welfare (IFAW). He has been studying sperm whales for over 20 years, first visiting the Azores as a student to investigate the traditional whaling industry there in the late 1970s, and even going to sea with the whalers to watch them at work. In the early 1980s, working on a WWF project with Dr Hal Whitehead, he helped to develop new visual and acoustic techniques for studying live sperm whales at sea. Returning to the Azores in 1987, with funding from IFAW, these methods were used to successfully promote whale watching as an alternative to traditional whaling and to continue investigations of these magnificent animals. He has also worked with sperm whales in New Zealand and the Caribbean.

Index

*Entries in **bold** indicate pictures*

Recommended Reading

Darling, J., Nicklin, C., Norris, K., Whitehead, H. and Wursig, B., *Whales, Dolphins and Porpoises*. National Geographic Book Division.

Evans, Peter G. H., *The Natural History of Whales and Dolphins*, (Natural History Series),

Leathewood, S., Reeves, R., *Sierra Club Handbook*.

Martin, A., *The Illustrated Encyclopedia of Whales and Dolphins*, Portland House.

Payne, Roger, *Among Whales*.

Whitehead, H., *Sail to the Whales*.